The CANADIAN Rockies

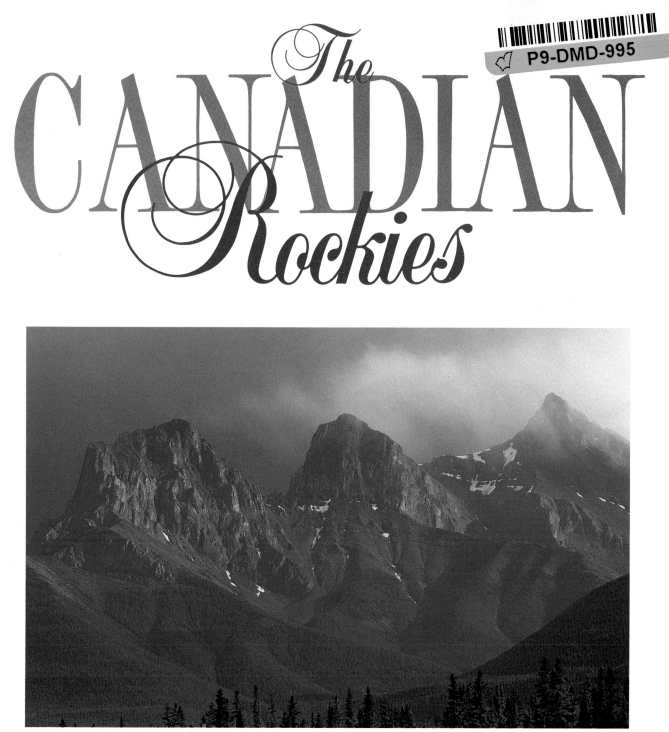

The Three Sisters, A Landmark in the Canmore Area

HIGH COUNTRY COLOUR

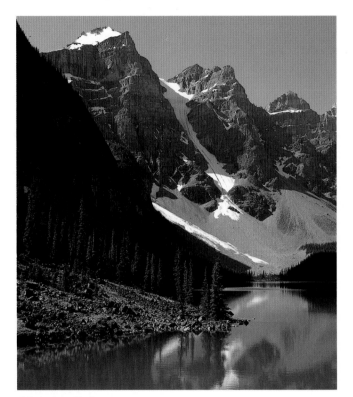

Moraine Lake

The "Shining Mountains"

The Canadian Rockies contain some of the most dramatic mountain scenery in the world! And all of it was once under water!

Although the Rocky Mountain chain extends from the Yukon Territories south to the Mexican border, the highest most spectacular peaks occur in Canada north of Vancouver. Today our Canadian Rockies, together with the more rounded peaks belonging to our southern neighbours, still remain rugged, unspoiled and little inhabited.

For at least 100,000 years, and perhaps many thousands more, Indian tribes called the "Shining Mountains" theirs. The name given by the Indians was recorded by the Verendrye brothers who came from France in 1742 to "discover" an area of the mountains in present-day Montana.

In the early 1700's, explorers returning from the North American continent mentioned an Indian people living in a country 'with fabled peaks reaching up to the sky!' The name "Rockies" seems to have been given first in French by an explorer called Leguardeur St. Pierre in 1752. In his diary, he aptly named them "Montagnes de roches" (Mountains of Rock).

A Never-Ending Journey

Before the CPR railroad opened up transportation, it took weeks of arduous trekking on foot or horseback to cross the mountains, in most cases, blazing your own trail as you went, and confronting both wild animals and surprised natives en route! The early explorers probably thought that the north-south chain of mountains would not be too wide and that there would be welcoming plains waiting on the far side. Such thinking probably kept them going!

Today's traveller heading west from the prairies may well believe that there is only one range of mountains to cross before reaching the Pacific Coast. The Rockies chain is the first of seven major north-south ranges separating the prairies from the Pacific Ocean.

Still, the Rockies are the most grandiose and awe-inspiring of the seven chains. Because Arctic air currents flow south over the Rockies between October and April, repelling the moist warmer air mass moving east from the Pacific, the Rockies' colder climate has attracted fewer inhabitants than the Pacific Coastal mountains. Thus they have remained relatively uninhabited.

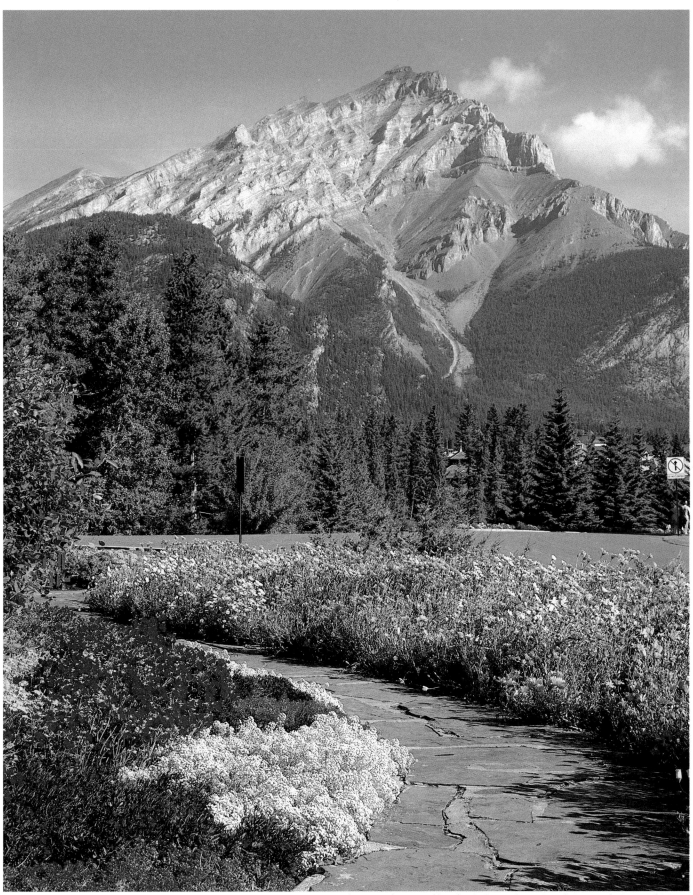

Above: The Banff Administration Gardens and Cascade Mt.
Following Page: The Banff Springs Hotel opened in 1888

The Mountains Rise Up

It took a mere 50 million years for the Rockies to form! The process actually began 600 million years ago in the late Precambrian when the western part of the continent, now Alberta and British Columbia, was totally submerged in a shallow sea. Over 500 million years, much sediment built up in this giant inland sea.

Two tectonic plates, that of the westward-pushing Canadian Shield and that of the eastward-pushing Pacific plate came together and began to push upward, so that land which had been under water was gradually forced upwards to form the mountains we know today.

Volcanic activity continued to shape the mountains until a "recent" ice age only 12,000 years ago gave the Rockies their "modern" shape with our familiar rivers and icefields.

Mineral Riches

The debris left behind from the slow upward shifting of the two continental plates contained fossil-rich marine sediments left over from the inland sea. The Rockies are also laden with ore of all kinds, especially gold, copper and silver, not to mention jade and more humble but important substances like coal. The quest for this mineral wealth continues to inspire many daring adventurers.

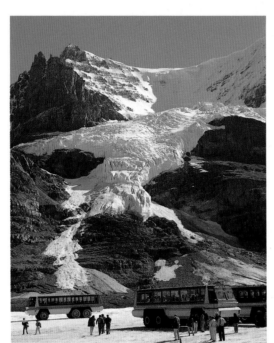

An Athabasca Glacier Tour

How the National Parks Began

Many square miles of the Canadian Rockies are now national parks or special forest reserves. People may not purchase land in the parks; however, Parks Canada leases the land within town sites such as Banff and Jasper. The story behind the founding of Canada's first national park is interesting. Three railroad workers, Thomas and William McCardell and their friend Frank McCabe, were exploring, intrigued by a strangely warm area in the Banff vicinity, now well-known as the Cave and Basin outside Banff, when they spotted steam issuing from a cleft in the rock. The water down below was incredibly warm and there was a heavy sulphurous smell in the air.

These adventurers clambered down into a hot pool which can be seen today just as it was in 1885. They had

a marvellous bath and came up feeling incredibly relaxed yet exhilarated!

Tourist Attraction

The three saw the potential and began bringing small groups of workers to the seductive spot. They tried to lay claim to their discovery only to have the grass cut from under their feet by the ambitious railroad president, Sir William Van Horne. He instantly realized that the "Magic Waters", long known as such to the Indians, could be a superb tourist attraction! "Since we can't export the scenery, we'll have to import the tourists!" he quipped, and proceeded to do just that, building a vast and incredibly elegant hotel, the Banff Springs Hotel, in the midst of dense wilderness! This hotel was the first in a chain of hotels undertaken by Van Horne. A 10 square-mile federal reserve, forerunner of Canada's first National Parks, was built around the springs. Two years later, a slightly larger area, 260 square miles, Rocky Mountain National Park, was set aside. The total size of Banff National Park today: 2564 square miles (4126 square kilometers).

And what about the intrepid discoverers of the springs who deserved the real credit? Surely they were richly rewarded for such a find? Van Horne convinced the Canadian government to step in and refuse their claim in his favour, buying them off with a paltry $900, and . . . the haying rights to a small adjacent area! The poor men protested, but to no avail.

People From Everywhere

Once the national parks came into being, along with the completion of the Canadian Pacific Railroad across Canada, people began arriving from many foreign lands. Some of the first were Swiss mountain climbers, who came out with the new railroad and began guiding other visitors. Many of them stayed to form the growing present-day community of third and fourth generation Swiss settlers in Western Canada.

Well-to-do Americans and European aristocrats were also lured by the elegant new Banff Springs Hotel completed in 1888, which contrasted dramatically with

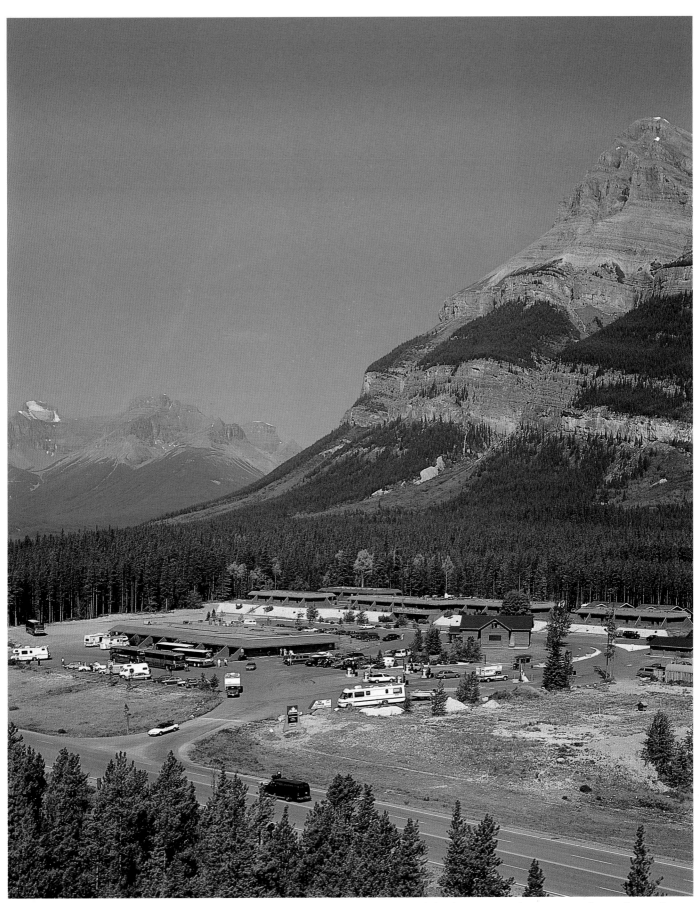

The Crossing, one of the largest service centers along the parkway

the untamed wilderness around it. At night, the brightly-lit hotel with the surrounding forest resembles a great passenger ship on a dark sea!

A group of Yale University students were the first to climb above 11,000 feet in the Canadian Rockies. The Yale-Lake Louise Club climbed Mountain Temple in 1894.

Then came a series of daring mountaineers, not only Swiss, but Austrian, British and North American. The Columbia Icefield was discovered in 1898 by two British climbers, Collie and Woolley.

In the "early" days before World War II, hiking or hunting in the Rockies was a true wilderness experience. According to renowned outfitter and writer, Andy Russell, people would be out on the trail with reliable guides for weeks on end and never smell civilization! Nowadays, people enter the Rockies at relatively high speed and "do" the excursions in a matter of hours or a few days at most, in keeping with today's accelerated life style.

A refuge From Civilization

While things aren't as pristine as they were 100 years ago, despite increasing numbers of visitors and local residents, the Rockies are still surprisingly clean! Everywhere on the hiking trails are large signs: "Pack out your garbage"! Somehow even the least respectful kind of people make an effort at this, perhaps because they sense the wonder of the place, unlike any other corner of North America in its grandiose beauty.

Nowadays, the Rockies' charm has become legendary throughout the world. Tourists come from the Far East, Japan and Hong Kong, from all over Europe and South America, Australia, etc., to enjoy the comfort of four and five-star hotels and the relatively unspoiled sights set up for tourists. Nonetheless, people who want to rough it, packing in their food and gear, can still do it all on foot and disappear from civilization for days and weeks on end, blissfully catching their own fish for dinner and eating berries for dessert to enjoy a feeling of "discovery" and elation similar to that of the early explorers.

Birds & Beasts, Flowers and Fossils!

Plant and animal varieties are in the hundreds in the Rockies. Visitors are not permitted to pick flowers lest they should become extinct, nor are they allowed to remove any undersea fossils they might find atop mountain peaks. Hunting is also forbidden in order to protect certain game which is already in decreasing supply. Constant pressure exists to develop the more accessible wilderness areas within the Parks. Yet it is the pristine untouched nature of the Rockies which attracts visitors and the variety of life forms found there.

There are elk, deer, moose, big horn sheep always appearing to perch precariously out on a ledge, rabbits, hare, funny little pikas, looking like out-of-focus rabbits, pristine white mountain goats, coyotes, beaver, many kinds of squirrel, wildcats and cougars, and most awesome of all Rocky mountain beasts, the grizzly bear. Elk and other horned animals when provoked can be menacing but the bear family, both brown and grizzly, are perhaps the only major threat to human beings, especially when hikers inadvertently get in between a mother and her cubs. While the grizzly is larger, weighing up to 800 lbs. as opposed to the 500 lb. maximum of the black bear, probably the black bear is more dangerous to humans because they are more likely to explore close to campsites and trails than the aloof grizzly. "Black" bears can in fact be sandy blond in colour, while grizzlies are usually dark brown; but they too may be blond occasionally!

Being There

Words and pictures can only give an impression of a beauty that defies description: hiking in the sharp, clean air, testing your body as you push yourself up steeper and steeper grades in search of the highest peak, and the accompanying feeling of exhilaration when you look out over a panorama of snow-capped peaks in front and below; the smell of new plants and warming earth emerging from winter; standing motionless watching a moose splashing through water, these things will reveal the real spirit of the "Shining Mountains". This book is a memento of such experiences.

A view of the Jasper Townsite from Whistlers Mountain

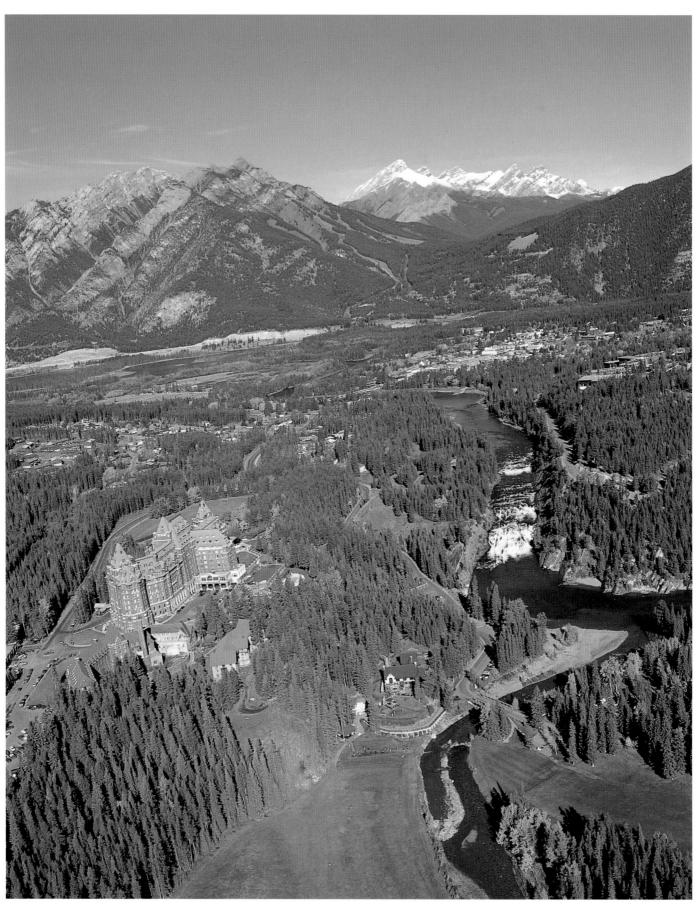

The Banff Springs Hotel and Bow Falls

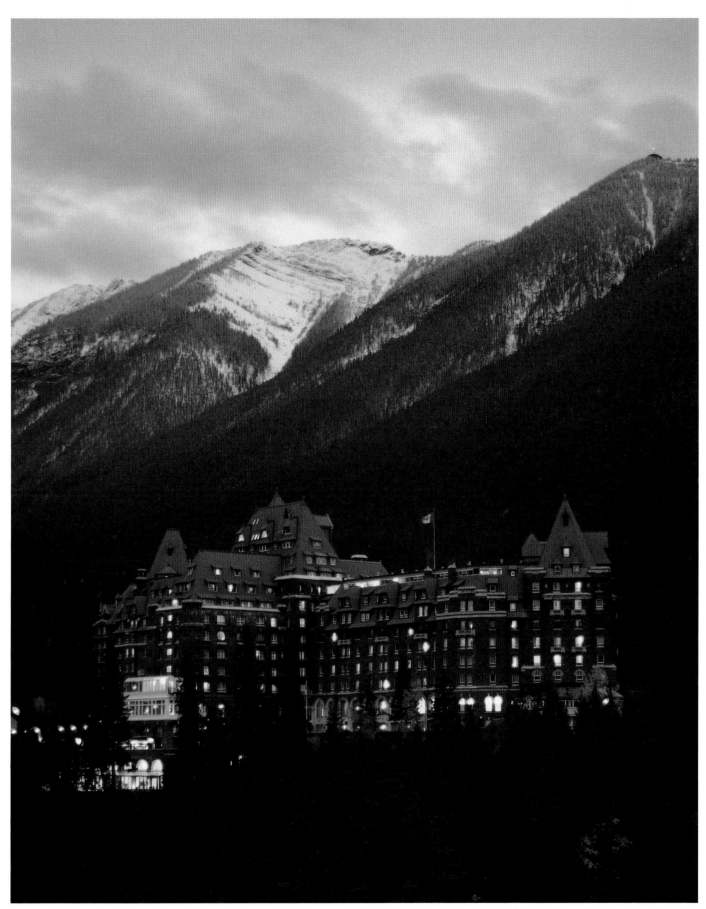

The evening lights of the Banff Springs Hotel

Mt. Rundle

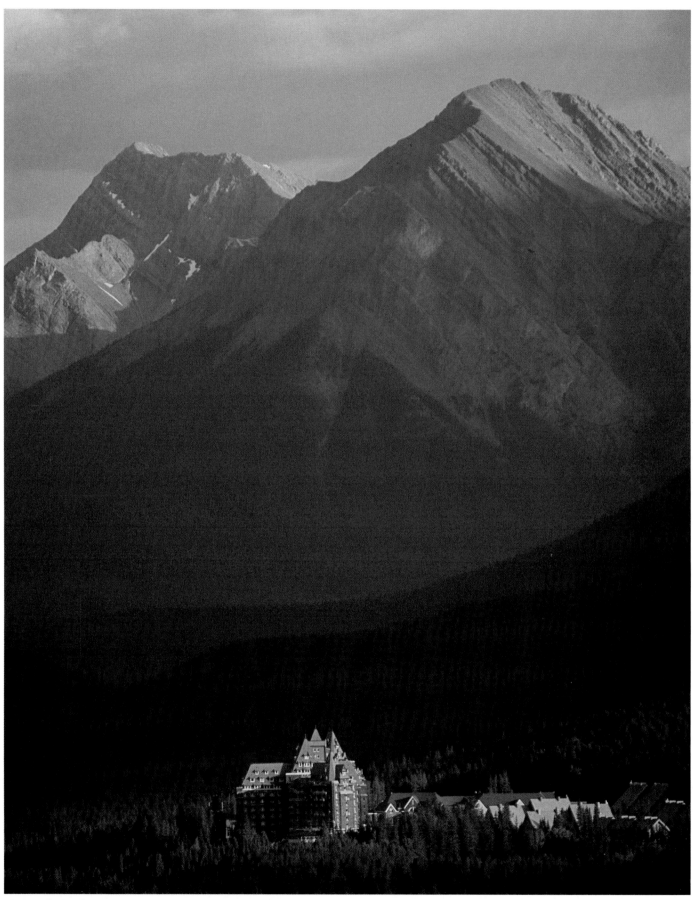

A Castle in the Rockies: The Banff Springs Hotel

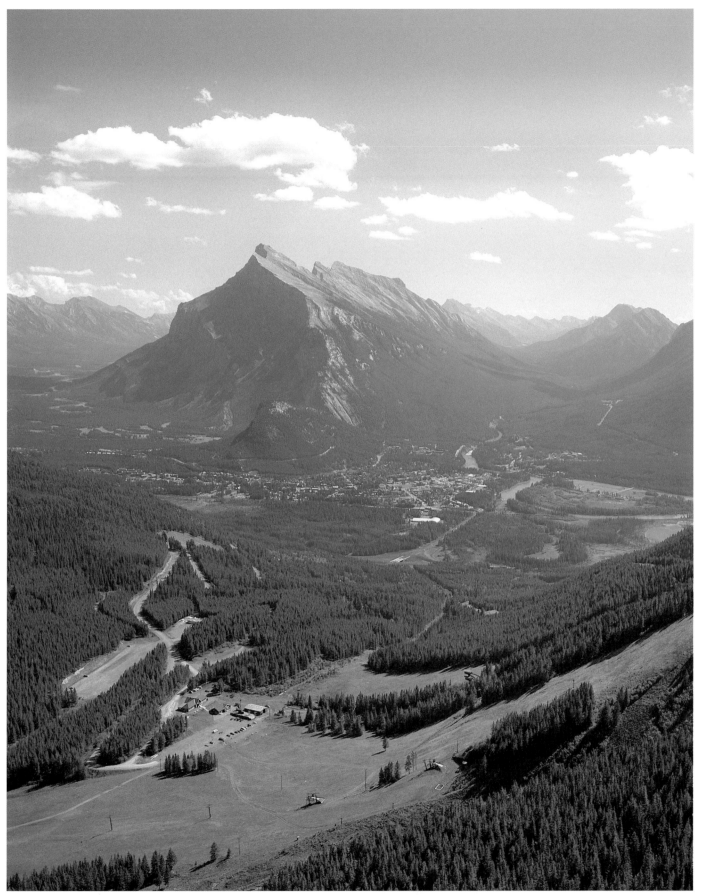

Mt. Rundle and The Banff Townsite from Mt Norquay

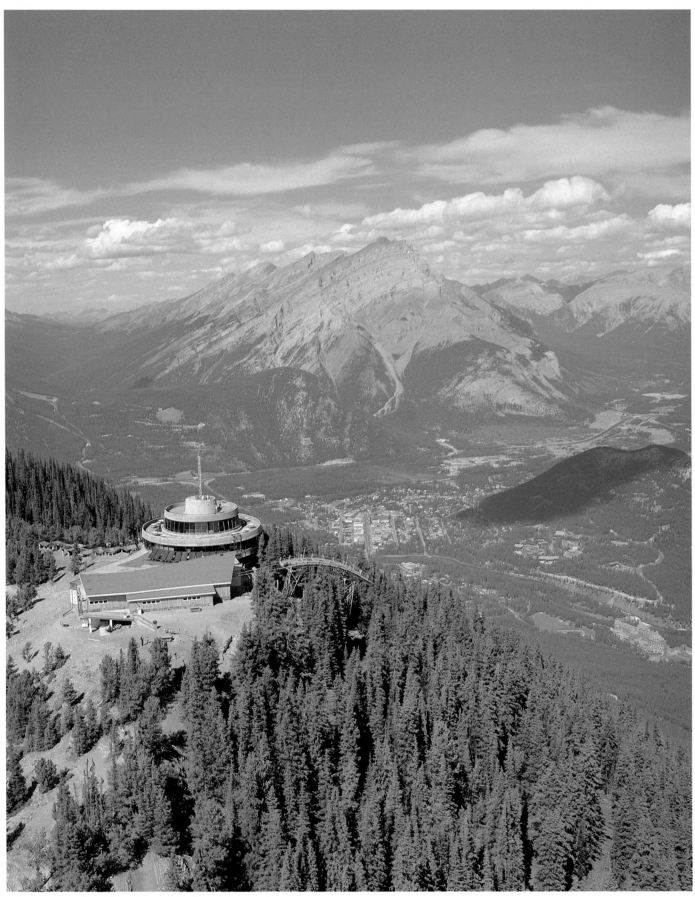

The spectacular view from Sulphur Mountain

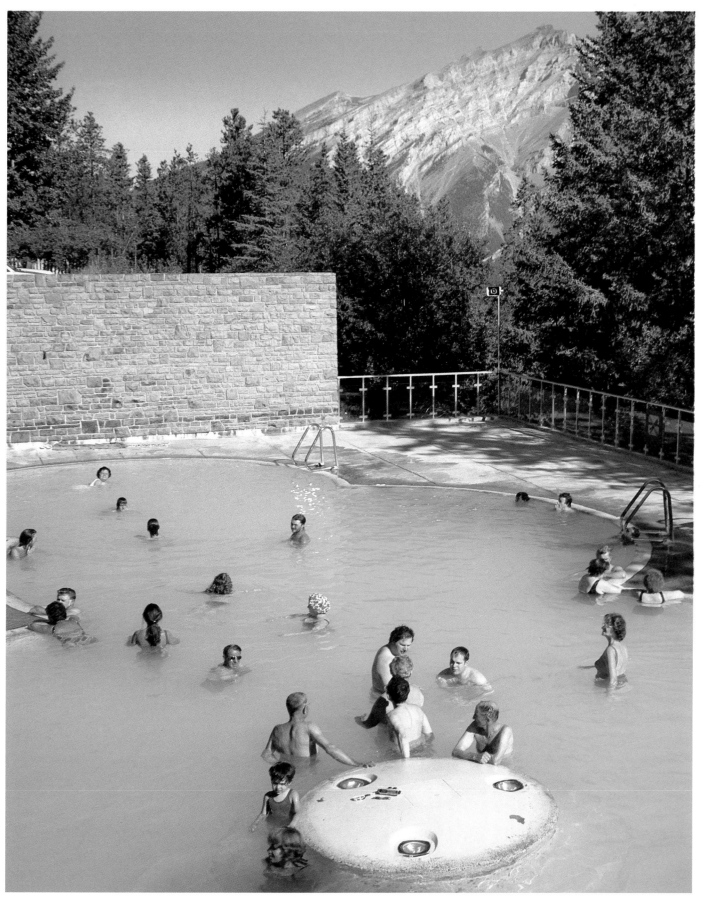

The Hot Springs Pool in Banff

The Cave and Basin

Johnston Canyon

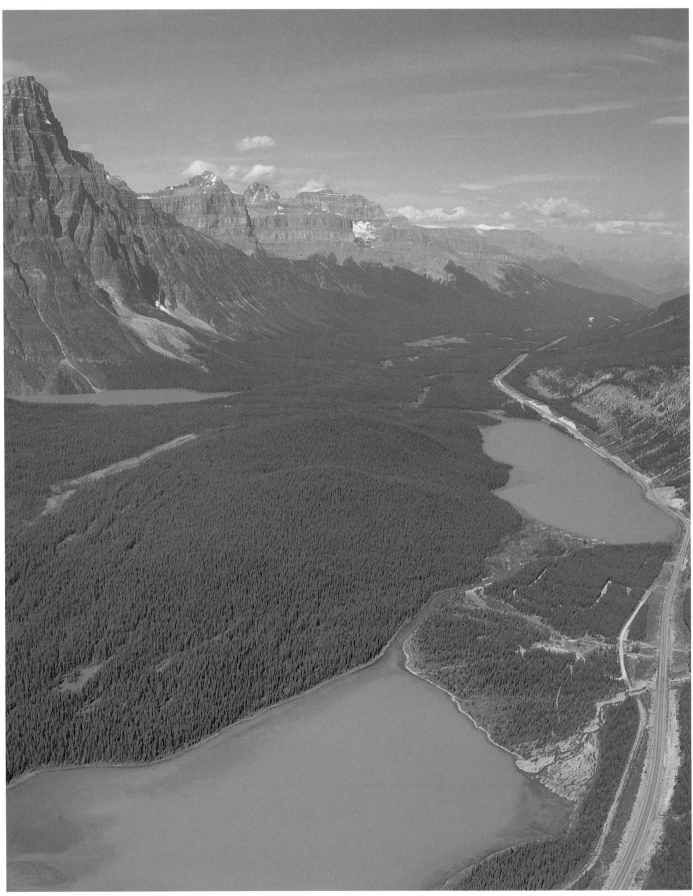

The Upper and Lower Waterfowl Lakes

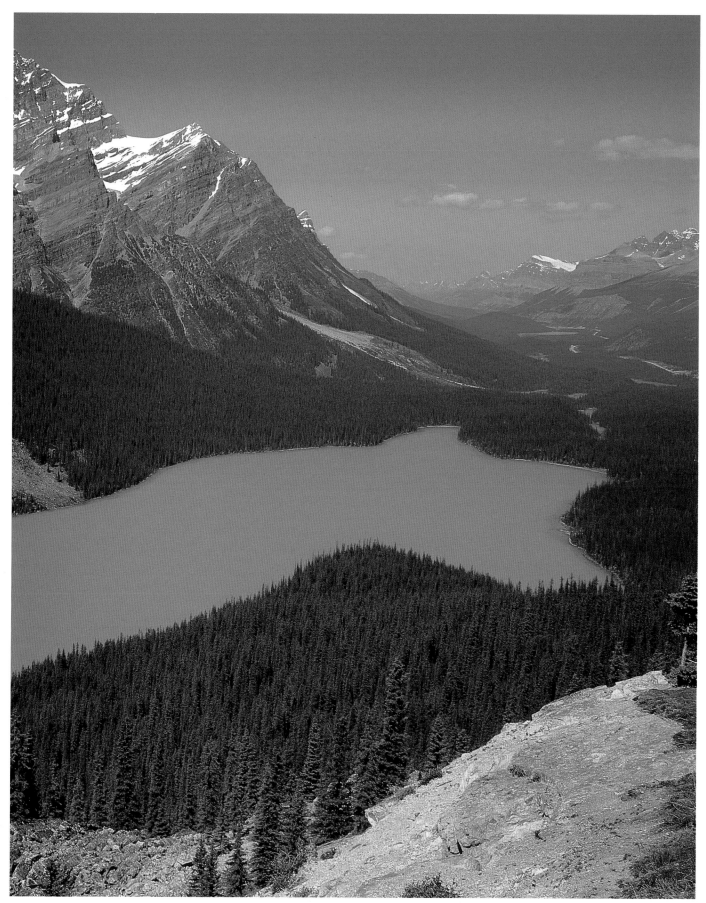

The Peyto Lake Viewpoint 1000ft. (305m) above the valley

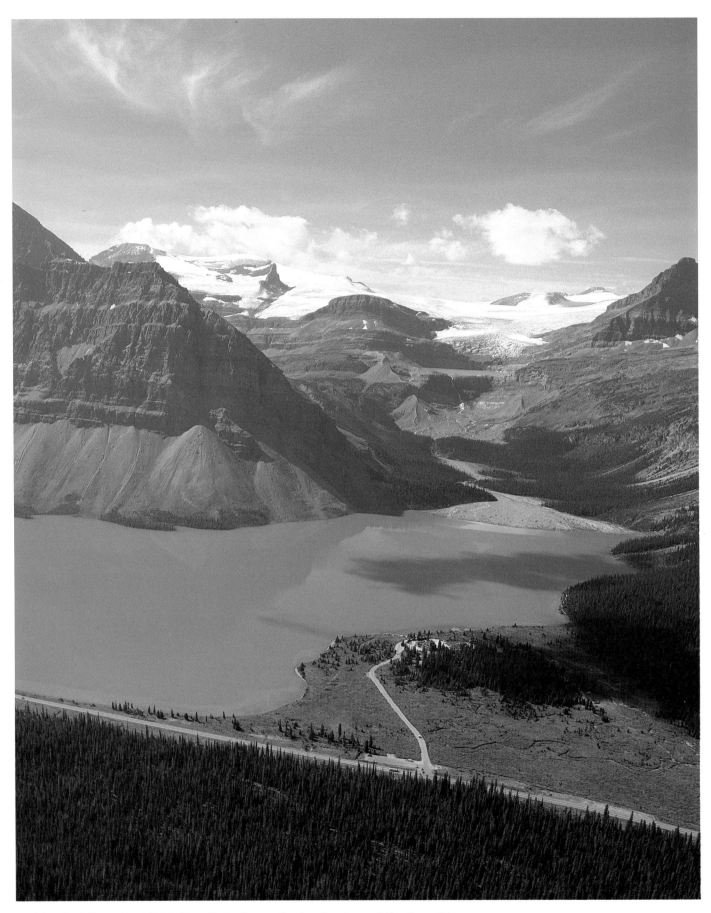

Fed by the Wapta Ice Field, Bow Lake forms the headwaters of the Bow River

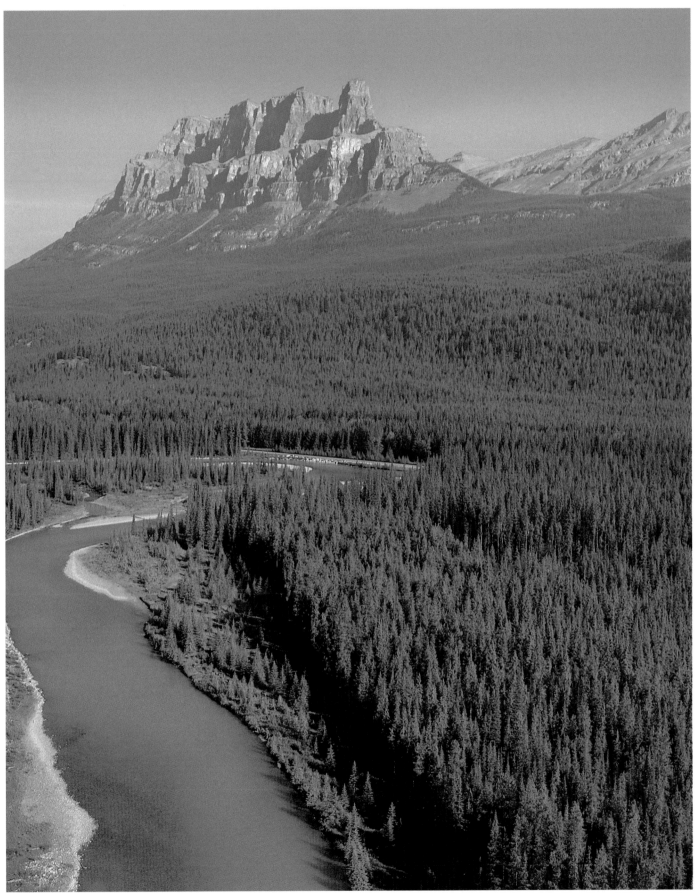

Castle Mountain: the most distinctive peak between Banff and Lake Louise

Lake Minnewanka

Above: Moose at a stream crossing
Following page: The Chateau at Lake Louise overlooks one of the most famous views in The Rockies

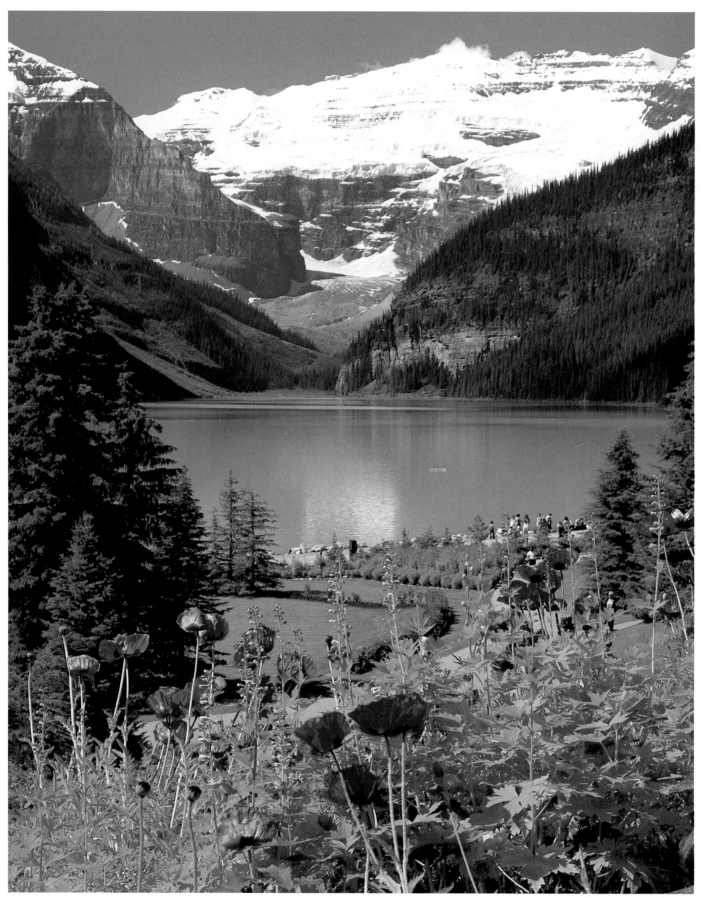

Lake Louise in full bloom

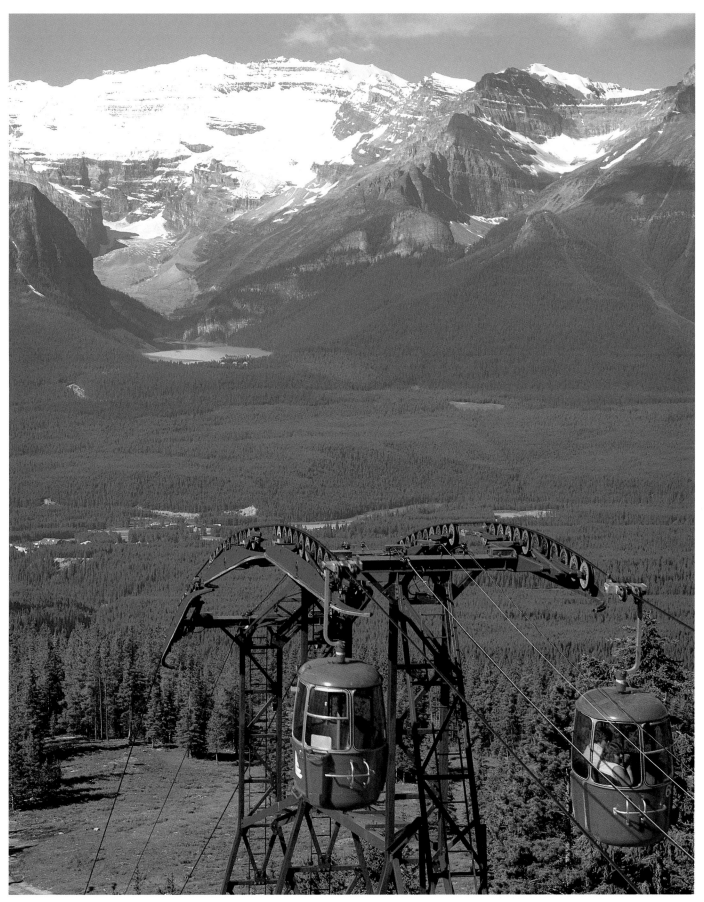

Gondola Cars at The Lake Louise ski area

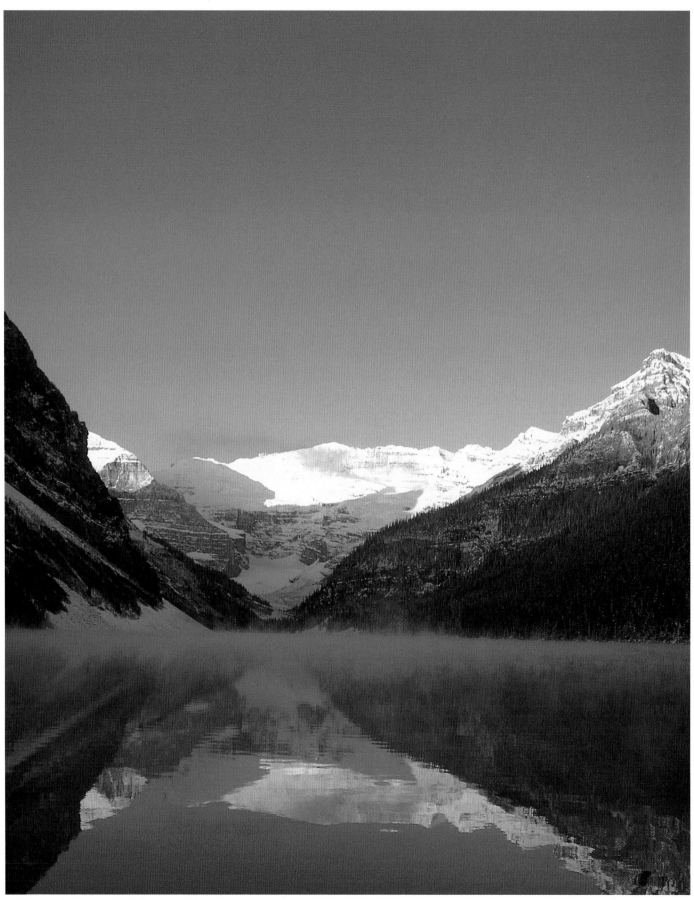

Lake Louise and The Victoria Glacier

Black Bear and Cubs

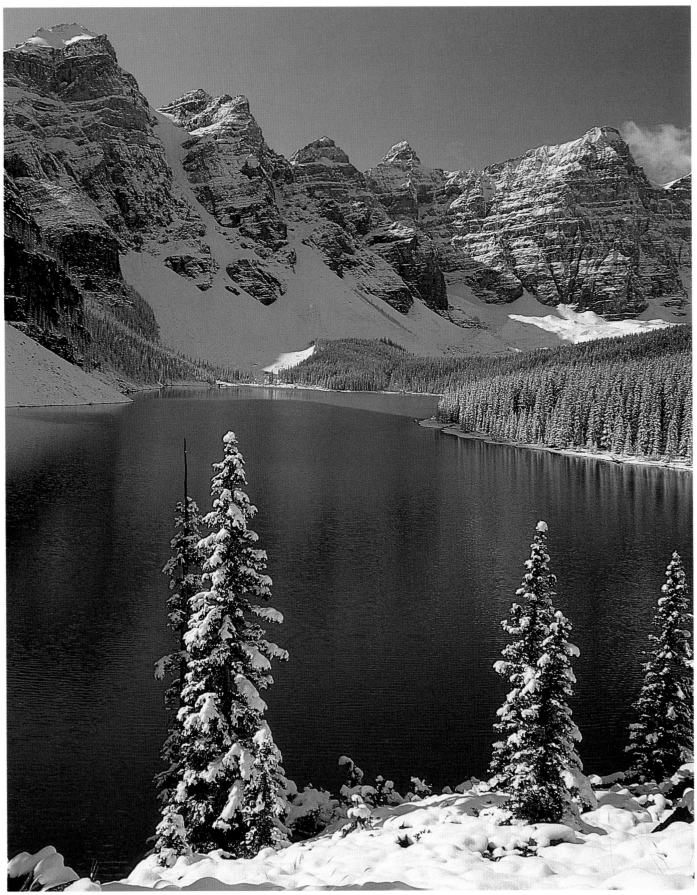

Moraine Lake in the Valley of Ten Peaks

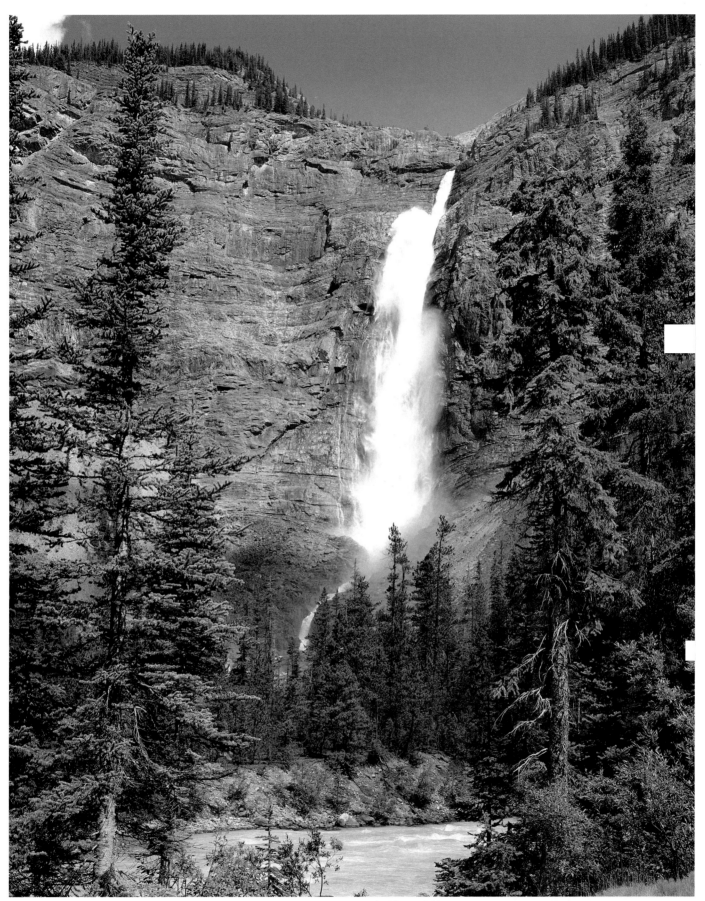

Takakkaw falls, The Highest Waterfall in Canada (380m)

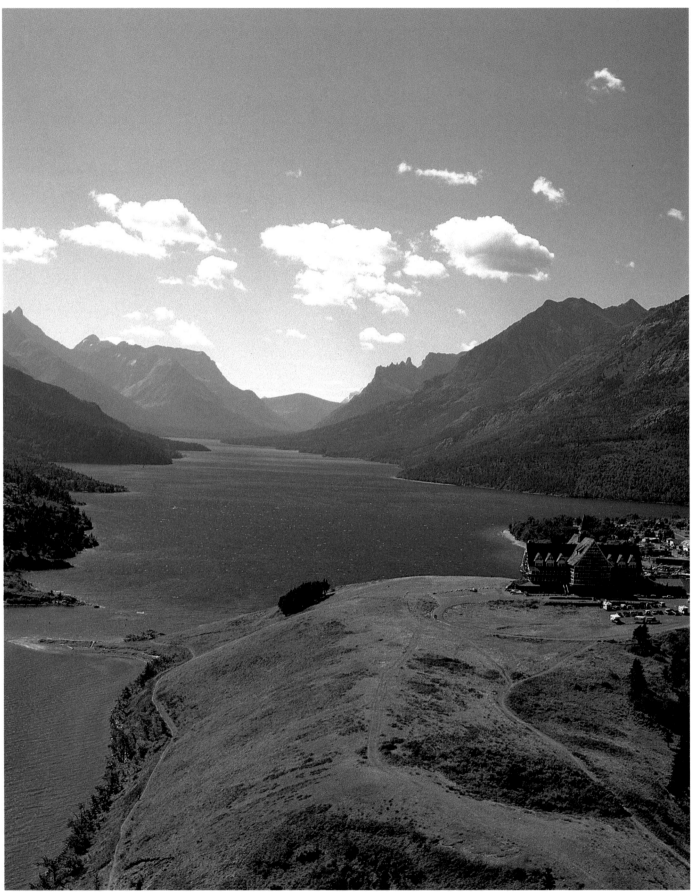

The Prince of Wales Hotel in Waterton Lakes

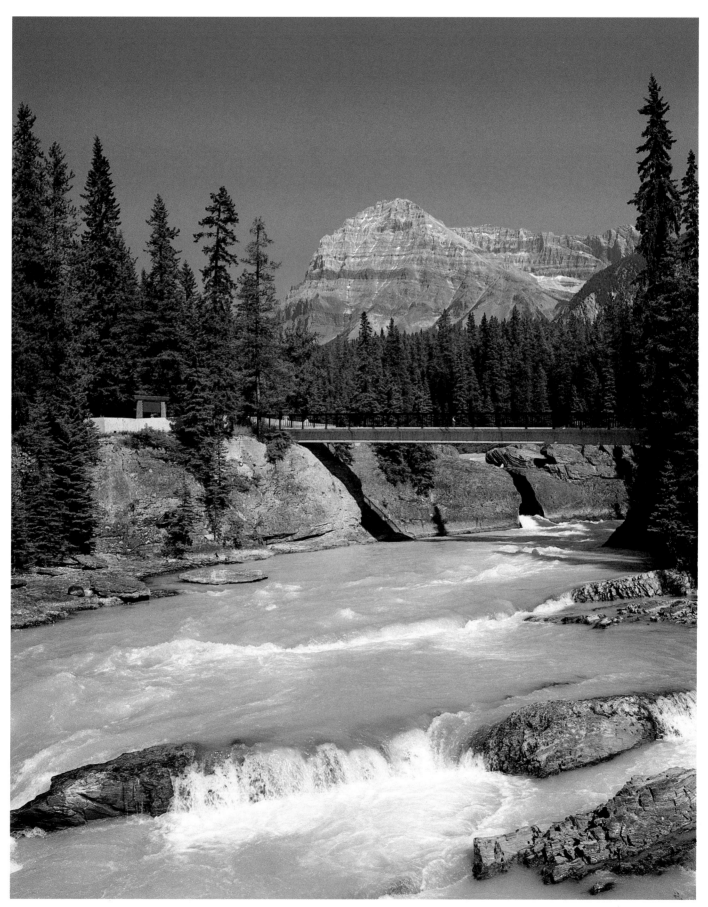

The Natural Bridge in Yoho National Park

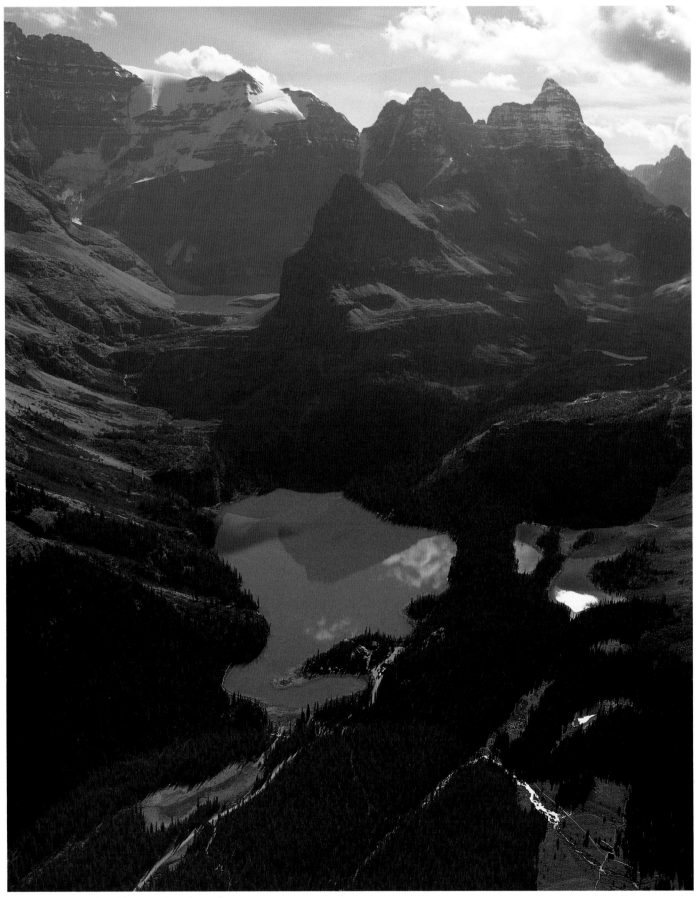

Lake O'hara in Yoho National Park

Emerald Lake

Twin Falls in Yoho National Park

Mountain Goat

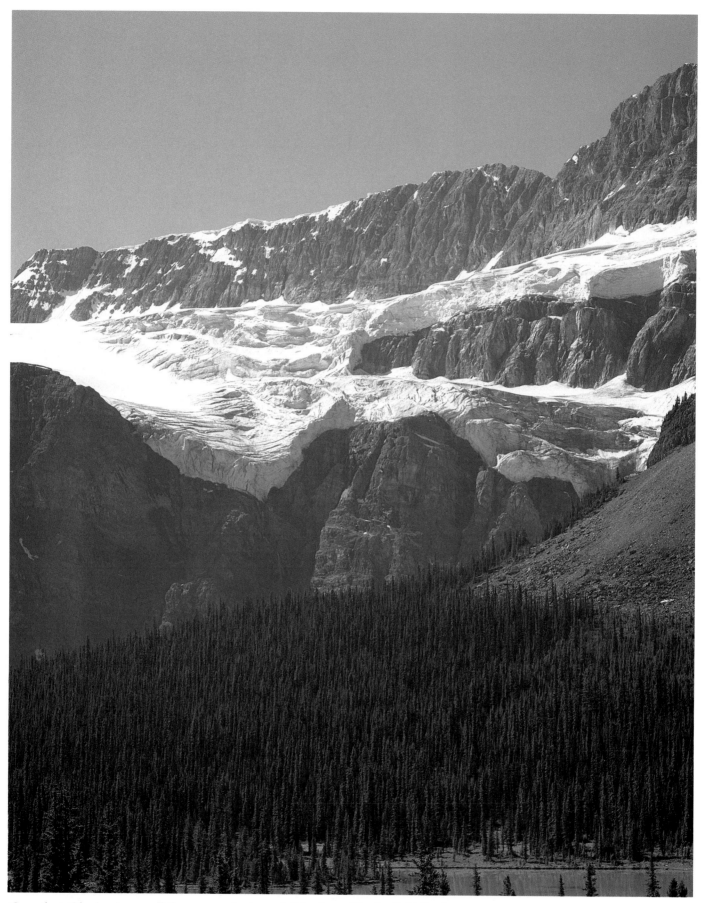

Crowfoot Glacier is one of the many glaciers visible from The Icefield Parkway

Above: Big Horn Sheep (RAM)
Following Page: Snow Coaches tour the immense Athabasca Glacier

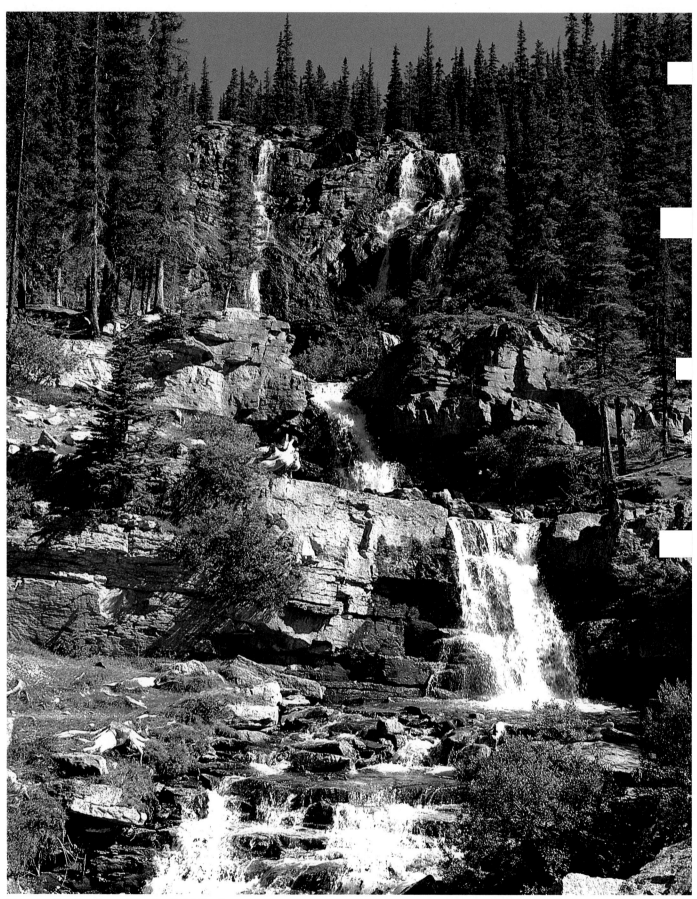

Tangle Creek, along The Icefield Parkway

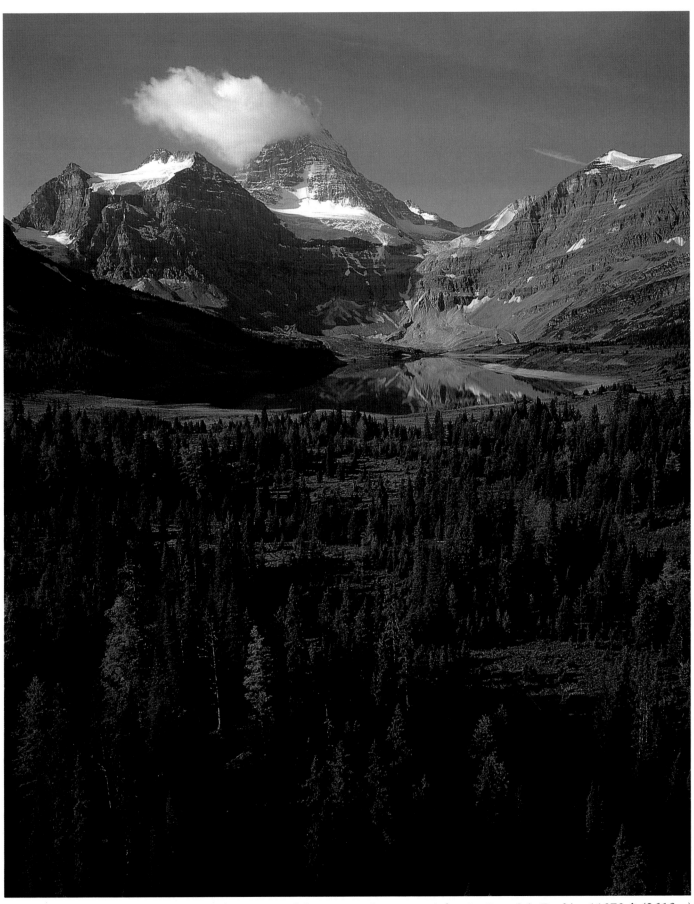

Mt. Assiniboine, one of the most unique mountains in Canada's Rockies 11870 ft (3618m)

Nigel Creek Falls

48

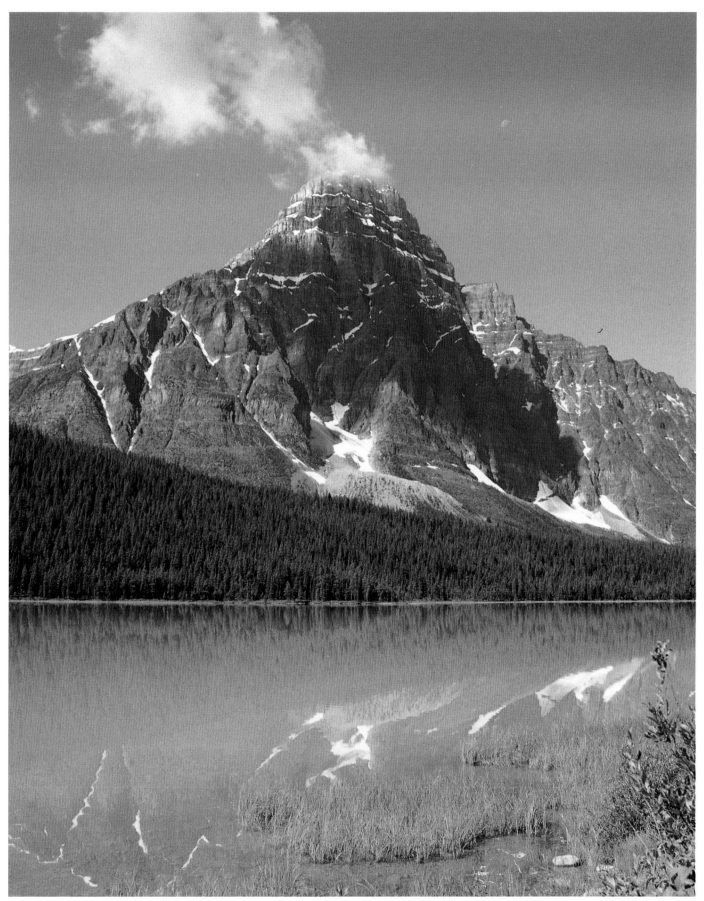

Mt. Chephren, along The Icefield Parkway

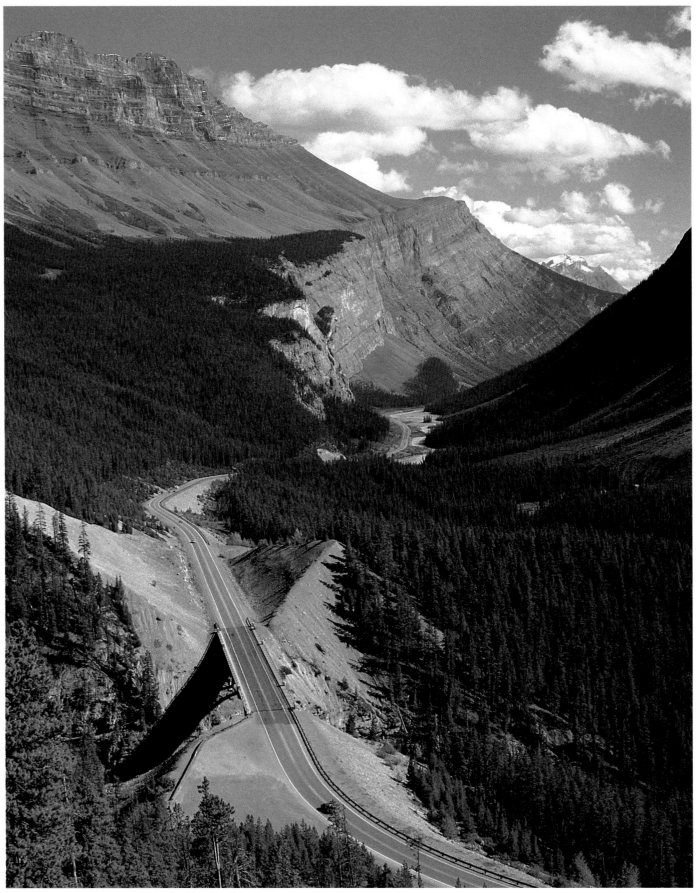

The Big Hill, as viewed along The Icefield Parkway

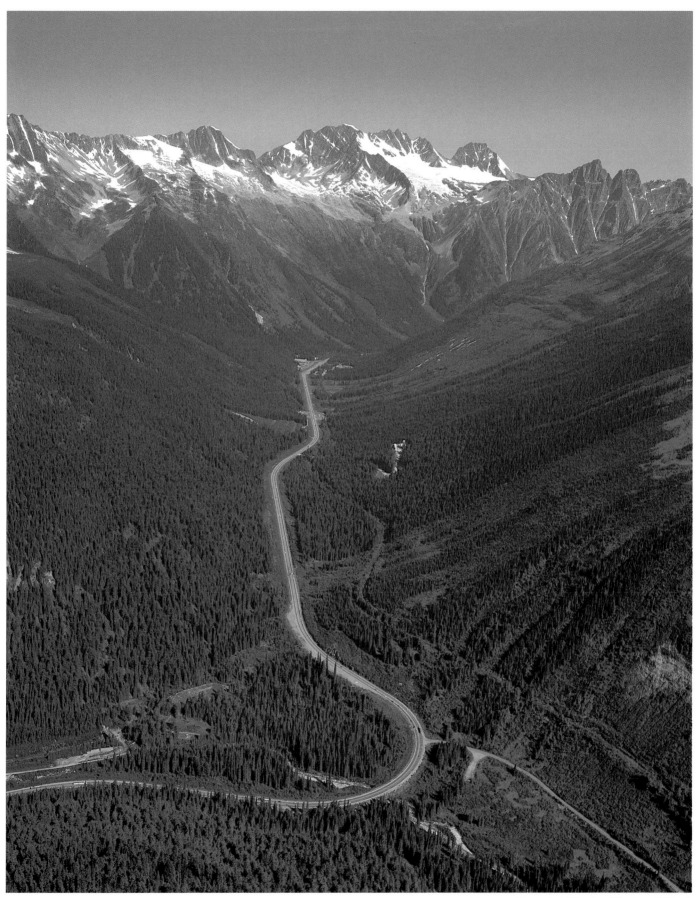

Rogers Pass in Glacier National Park

A Grizzly and Cub, year-round residents of Canada's Parks

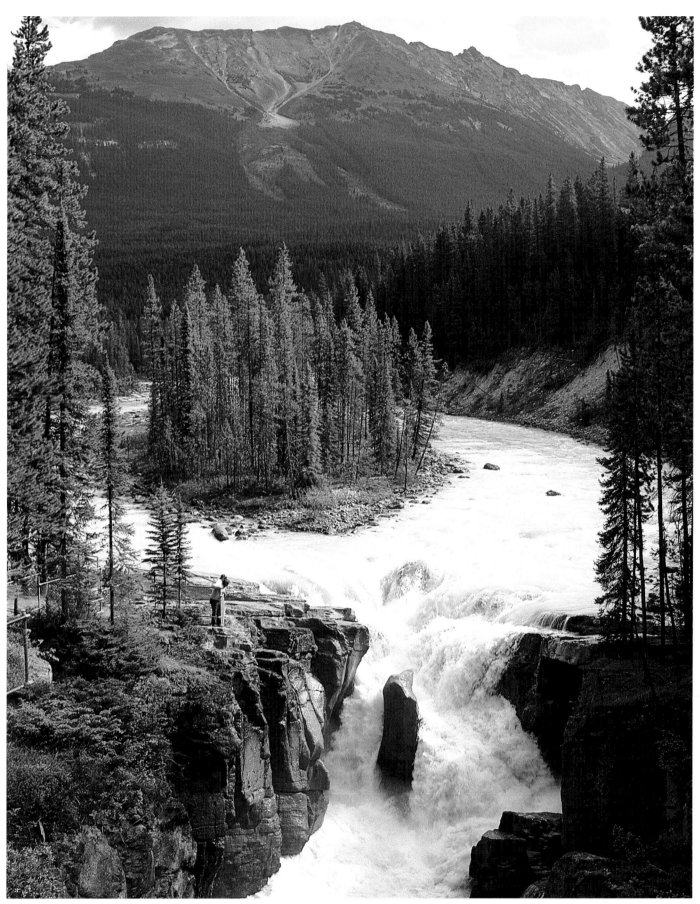

Sunwapta falls, Jasper National Park

The Jasper Park Lodge

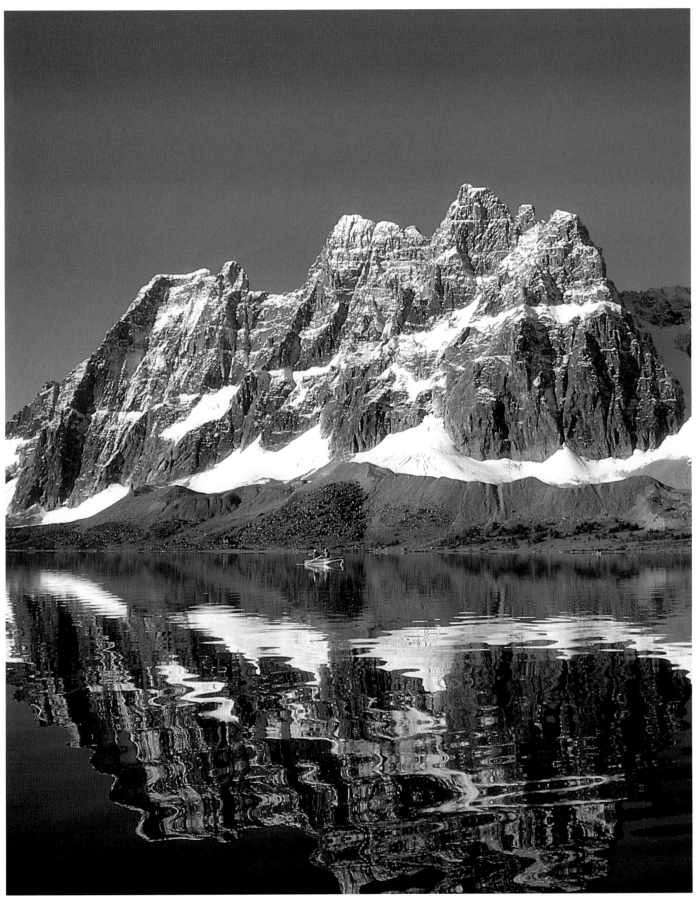

Tonquin Valley, Jasper National Park

The Jasper Tramway on Whistlers Mountain

Lifting visitors to the summit of Whistlers Mountain, The Tramway offers spectacular views of Jasper and area

Mt. Edith Cavell, Jasper National Park

Above: WAPITI (ELK)
Following Page: Maligne Lake and Spirit Island, Jasper National Park

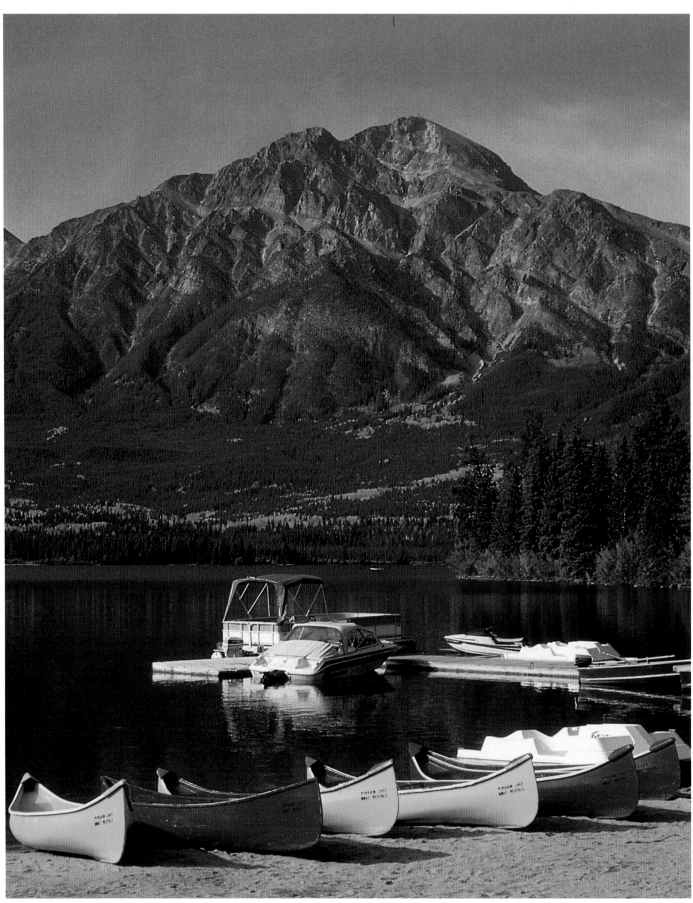

Pyramid Mountain, Jasper National Park

Banff Main Street

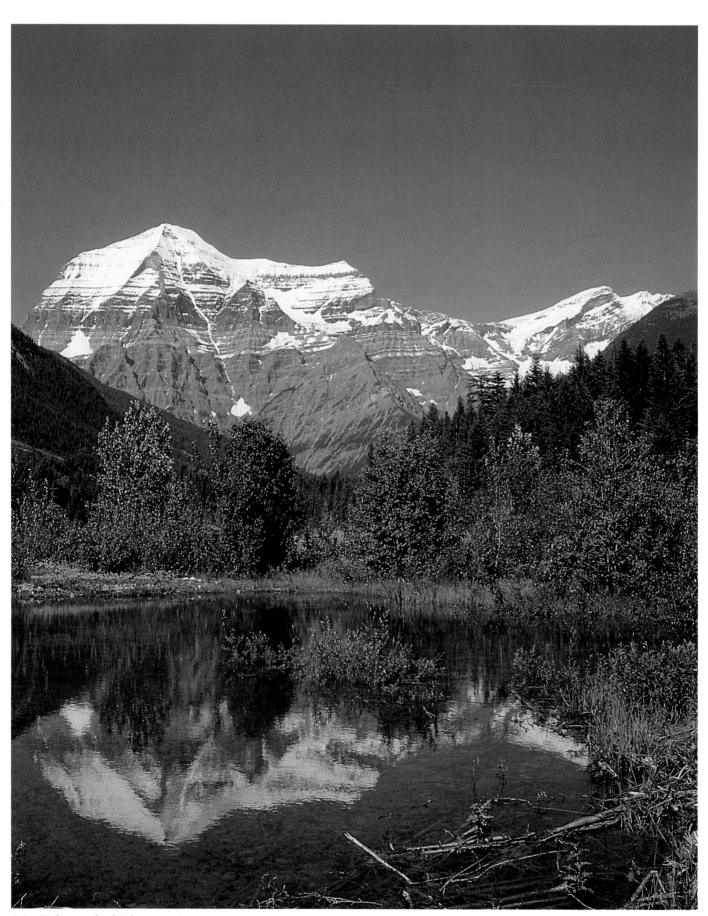

Mt. Robson, the highest peak in the Canadian Rockies 12972 ft. (3954m) and one of the highest peaks in the world. The Indian Name (Yuh-Hai-Has-Kun) means "The Mountain of the Spiral Road"